KENWOOD

creative
food processor

cooking

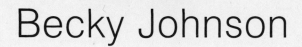

Becky Johnson

SIMON & SCHUSTER
A CBS COMPANY

First published in Great Britain by Simon & Schuster UK Ltd, 2001
A CBS Company

Copyright © Kenwood Ltd, 2001

20 19 18 17 16 15 14

Simon & Schuster UK Ltd
222 Gray's Inn Road
London
WC1X 8HB

Text design: Barry Lowenhoff
Typeset by Stylize Digital Artwork
Photography by Steve Baxter
Food preparation by Jane Stevenson
Styling by Marian Price
Printed and bound in China

A CIP catalogue record for this book is available from the
British Library

ISBN 0 85941 994 0

Recipe notes

All recipes in this book give ingredients in both metric (g, ml, etc.)
and imperial (oz, pints, etc.) measures. Use either set of quantities,
but not a mixture of both, in any one recipe.

All teaspoons and tablespoons are level, unless otherwise stated.
1 teaspoon = a 5 ml spoon.
1 tablespoon = a 15 ml spoon.
Egg size is medium unless otherwise stated.
Vegetables and fruit are medium-size unless otherwise stated.

PREPARATION AND COOKING TIMES

Preparation and cooking times are included as a general guide;
preparation times especially are approximate and timings are
usually rounded to the nearest 5 minutes.

Preparation times include the time taken to prepare ingredients
in the list, but not to make any basic recipe.

The cooking times given at the head of the recipes are periods
when the dish can be left largely unattended. e.g. baking, and not
the total amount of cooking time for the recipe. Always read and
follow the timings given for the steps of the recipe in the method.

RAW EGGS

The Cookies and Cream Ice Cream on page 47 contains raw eggs.
For any dish containing raw eggs, make sure you use eggs which
are as fresh as possible. Pregnant women, small children and
people susceptible to infection should avoid lightly cooked eggs
and dishes containing raw eggs.

contents

introduction 4

the attachments 6

using your food processor to make... 8

a–z of how to prepare foods 10

basic recipes 12

soups, salads and snacks 22

meat and poultry 30

fish and shellfish 36

vegetables 40

cakes and desserts 46

breads 58

index 64

introduction

Welcome to your new Kenwood Food Processor and to an exciting new range of cooking possibilities. Whether you would like to get food on the table quicker, to make difficult recipes easier or need a little help with those boring, repetitive cooking jobs, then you need look no further than your Kenwood Food Processor.

The Kenwood can make light work of so many recipes – it will make old favourites even easier to prepare and inspire you to try a variety of new dishes, too.

The pace of life is so fast nowadays that it's hard to make sure we eat the balanced diet that's needed to keep us healthy and our energy levels high. The Kenwood Food Processor chops, slices and grates fruits and vegetables so efficiently that you can whip up healthy, colourful stir-fries, crunchy salads and fresh fruit puds in no time. All the recipes that usually take hours of preparation can be made in minutes – leaving you the time to really enjoy eating them!

The Kenwood Food Processor takes the hard work out of making bread, doing all the kneading for you in seconds and giving the lightest results. It can whizz up a quick, short, flaky pastry. It can blend soups in seconds, purée fruits and vegetables for exotic coulis or baby food and make delicious smoothies, fresh juices and cocktails that you'd normally pay a fortune for.

This book is a supplement to the instruction manual. It is meant to give you ideas and reliable, tested recipes to try. The first chapter includes basic recipes that can be used for a variety of different dishes, for example shortcrust pastry which can be used in recipes from apple pie to Cornish pasties. Later on in the book there are recipes that refer back to these basics such as the Courgette, Cheddar and Dijon Tart (page 27).

There are over 40 recipes created just for this book and they are divided into chapters just like a standard cookery book. So, you can refer to whichever you require with ease – if it's a quick bite you want, then turn to Soups, Salads and Snacks, page 22, or perhaps you want an easy pud – then check out Cakes and Desserts, page 46. The recipes come from all over the world, use a wide range of ingredients and vary from the very simple to the more involved. They are designed to illustrate the versatility of the Kenwood Food Processor and to fuel your imagination to experiment yourself, perhaps using a sauce from one of the recipes with a dish of your own creation. Whatever you choose to make in your Kenwood Food Processor we hope you have fun and many a pleasurable hour spent eating the results. Bon Appetit!

using your food processor

Your Kenwood Food Processor is designed to be easy and safe to use. To get the most from it and ensure you are using it correctly, it is best to read through your instruction manual before you use the machine. This way you'll have an idea of its scope so that you don't overload it and risk damaging the motor. It also includes instructions on how to fit the different attachments. Lastly, it explains all about the other built-in safety features, such as bowl lid interlock, and good, safe procedures for use.

It is important to remember that the knife blade and slicing discs are very sharp and should always be kept out of reach of children. To avoid accidents always remove the knife blade before tipping food out of the bowl. Never leave the blade in the sink – it's best to rinse it straight after use or put it into the dishwasher to prevent accidents occurring.

the attachments

Basic Attachments
These two attachments come as standard with all Kenwood Food Processors.

KNIFE BLADE   This is the attachment that you will probably use most often. It can be used for mixing, chopping, mincing, mashing, puréeing and rubbing in.

THICK SLICING/COARSE SHREDDING DISC   A reversible disc with slicing on one side and shredding on the other. For slicing vegetables and shredding and grating a wide range of foods.

Optional Attachments
DOUGH TOOL   Used to mix and knead yeasted recipes.

TWIN BEATER GEARED WHISK   Used to whisk egg whites, whip cream and whisk eggs and sugar for fatless sponges.

MAXI-BLEND CANOPY   Used in conjunction with the knife blade to blend soups.

THIN SLICING/FINE SHREDDING DISC   A reversible disc with slicing on one side and shredding on the other. For slicing vegetables finely and grating crisp fruit, vegetables and cheese.

STANDARD CHIPPER DISC   For making continental-style chips from potatoes or other root vegetables.

FINE 'JULIENNE-STYLE' CHIPPER DISC   For super-slim French fries or fine strips of root or other crisp vegetables.

RASPING DISC   For grating parmesan and other hard cheeses. (Popular in Germany and Austria for making potato dumplings.)

EXTRA-COARSE SHREDDING DISC   For grating vegetables and fruit really coarsely for salads. Also for grating cheese.

LIQUIDISER   For blending soups and sauces, making smoothies, milkshakes, cocktails and purées.

MULTI-MILL   For making baby food or small quantities of purées, grinding coffee beans and spices, and chopping herbs and nuts.

MINI-PROCESSOR BOWL   For making baby food, sauces or small quantities of purées and chopping herbs and nuts.

CITRUS PRESS   For juicing oranges, lemons, grapefruits and limes.

CENTRIFUGAL JUICER   For juicing hard fruits, such as apples, and vegetables, such as carrots.

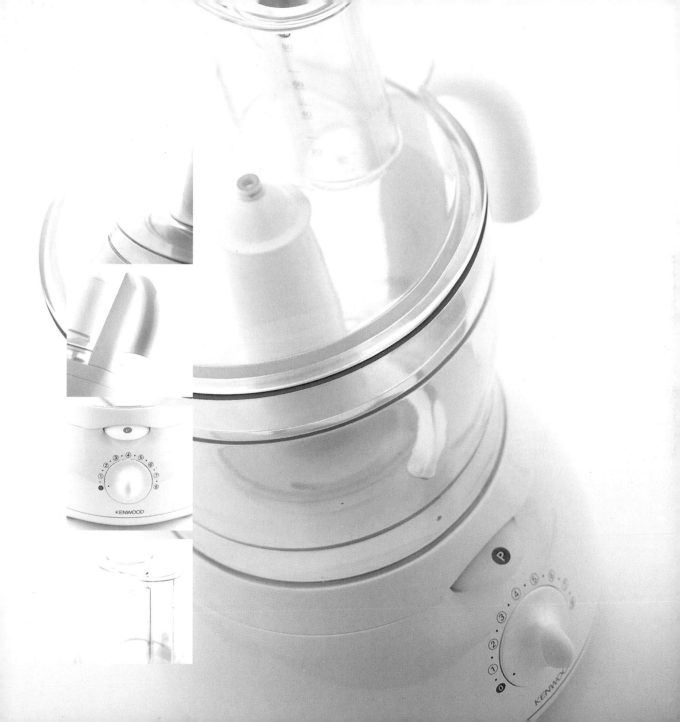

using your food processor to make...

BREAD AND OTHER YEAST DOUGHS If you have one, use the dough tool as it gives the best results. Otherwise use the knife blade.

▲ Place the flour, fat and other dry ingredients in the bowl and process for a few seconds to mix.

▲ With the machine running add the liquid mixture down the feed tube.

▲ Continue processing until the mixture forms a dough and becomes smooth in appearance and elastic to the touch – this will take 40–60 seconds. Allow the dough to rise then re-knead by hand.

BATTERS With the knife blade in position, place the dry ingredients, egg and a little liquid in the bowl. Process until smooth. Add the remaining liquid down the feed tube whilst the machine is operating.

CAKE MAKING Sponge-type cakes are best made by the all-in-one method. Always use a 'soft tub' margarine.

▲ All the ingredients are placed into the bowl.

▲ Process until smooth – approximately 10 seconds.

FRUIT CAKES Fruit cakes can be made by the creaming method. Always use a 'block' margarine straight from the refrigerator, cut into 2 cm/¾ in cubes.

Use the pulse to incorporate the fruit and take care not to overprocess as this may chop the fruit.

FRUIT COULIS, PURÉES AND SAUCES Soft fruits, such as summer berries, kiwi fruit, de-stoned mangoes and peaches can be puréed in the bowl with the knife blade in a few seconds. Add sugar and/or cream if required.

Hard fruits such as apples and pears or apricots, plums and rhubarb can all be cooked with a little water and sugar, if required, until tender and then puréed in the bowl with the knife blade in a few seconds.

GARLIC BUTTER Chop the garlic, then add the butter to the bowl with the knife blade fitted. Process until mixed thoroughly. You can also make other flavoured butters by adding chopped fresh herbs and/or spices.

ICE CREAMS AND SORBETS
Use the knife blade to process ice creams or sorbets two or three times during freezing to break down the large ice crystals and to give a smoother texture.

ICE LOLLIES Make fruit purées and freeze in ice cube trays or ice lolly moulds for healthy summer treats.

MAYONNAISE Place the egg and seasonings in the bowl. Process for a few seconds, then with the machine still running, gradually pour the oil down the feed tube in a slow steady stream.

MILKSHAKES AND SMOOTHIES These can be made quickly in the bowl with the knife blade or in the liquidiser. Just add milk or yogurt, fresh fruit and ice cream and whizz until smooth and frothy.

PESTO Put fresh basil leaves, toasted pine kernels, a peeled, chopped garlic clove, some olive oil and a little salt in the bowl with the knife blade. Process to a coarse paste. Add some grated Parmesan and a little water and process again.

SAVOURY DIPS Blend mixtures of cream cheese or yogurt with vegetables, spices and fresh herbs in the processor bowl fitted with the knife blade.

SHORTCRUST PASTRY AND SCONES

▲ Put the flour into the bowl. Use fat straight from the fridge and cut into 2 cm/¾ in cubes.

▲ Process until the mixture resembles fine breadcrumbs, but take care not to overprocess. Leave the machine running and add the liquid down the feed tube. Process until one or two balls of pastry are formed. Chill before use.

SOUPS Purée soups either before or after cooking. If before cooking, use the knife blade to process vegetables with a little liquid.

▲ If after cooking, drain the ingredients and place in the bowl with a little liquid from the pan.

▲ Process until the desired consistency has been reached, then add the purée to the remainder of the liquid in the pan.

VEGETABLE PURÉES
Place cooked vegetables in the processor bowl with the knife blade, add a little seasoning and some butter and/or milk or cream and process for a few seconds until smooth.

VINAIGRETTE DRESSINGS
Put all the ingredients in the bowl with the knife blade and process for a few seconds to give a smooth dressing.

a-z of how to prepare foods

APPLES   Peel apples (optional), quarter and core, then slice or grate by pushing down the larger feed tube onto the slicing/shredding disc.

BANANAS   Peel and use pusher to push down the feed tube with the motor running onto the slicing disc, or mash for baby food in the bowl with the knife blade.

BISCUITS   Chop biscuits, such as digestives or amaretti, in seconds in the processor fitted with the knife blade.

BREADCRUMBS   These can be made with the knife blade. The length of time processed will determine the degree of fineness.

CABBAGE   Trim and remove the core. Cut into pieces to fit in the feed tube. With the motor running, press down with the pusher onto the slicing disc. Use in coleslaws, salads, stir-fries or pasty fillings.

CANDIED PEEL   Add a little flour to the candied peel to stop the peel sticking to the blade and the bowl. Chop with the knife blade.

CARROTS   To slice carrots, use the slicing disc.

▲ Load the carrots vertically into the feed tube.

▲ If you have only one carrot to slice use the small feed tube. Load the carrot vertically as before.

▲ Both loading methods produce neat round slices. Or use the 'Julienne-style' chipper disc.

▲ Peel the carrots, cut into short lengths and load into the feed tube horizontally.

▲ The 'Julienne-style' chipper disc produces fine strips as shown here.

Or grate carrots with the shredding disc.

CELERIAC   Peel and cut into pieces small enough to fit down the feed tube. Use the chipper disc to make chips.

CELERY   Load the celery into the feed tube, end first, to slice.

CHEESE   Grate or slice hard cheeses with the slicing/shredding discs. Or chop using the knife blade.

CHILLIES   Chop fresh de-seeded chillies by dropping them through the feed tube with the motor running and the knife blade fitted.

COURGETTES   Process as for carrots. When slicing, whole pieces of courgette will give rounds, halves will give half moons.

CUCUMBERS   For slices, use the slicing/shredding disc. Cut the cucumber into short lengths. Whole pieces of cucumber will give thin rounds, halves will give half moons. Or, for fine strips, use the 'Julienne-style' chipper disc. Lay the cucumber pieces on their sides in the feed tube.

EGGS   Hard-boil eggs before chopping finely with the knife blade.

FENNEL BULBS   Process as for onions. To keep a good texture during cooking use the thick slicing disc.

GARLIC   Chop individual cloves of garlic with the knife blade. Peel and drop them down the feed tube with the motor running at high speed.

HERBS   Always make sure that herbs are washed and dried before processing. Remove any tough stalks from woody herbs such as thyme and rosemary. Chop in the mini-processor bowl or multi-mill.

LEEKS   For slices, use the slicing disc. Load the leeks vertically into the feed tube.

MEAT   For recipes which require mince, chop finely using the knife blade. First remove any bones or gristle and cut into 2.5 cm (1-inch) pieces. Chop in the bowl to the desired consistency.

MUSHROOMS   Wash and dry the mushrooms, then fill the feed tube with as many as possible. Use the slicing/shredding disc to slice them.

NUTS   Remove the shells and skins if they are bitter (this is easier to do if you blanch the nuts for 10 seconds in boiling water). Put the nuts in the bowl with the knife blade, or in the multi-mill or mini-processor bowl, and chop the nuts to the desired fineness. Check the nuts frequently to see how chopped they are.

ONIONS   Peel and cut into quarters. Push down the feed tube with the pusher onto the slicing/shredding disc. Alternatively, cut in half, place in the bowl and chop with the knife blade.

PARSNIPS   Roughly chop peeled parsnips using the knife blade. Using the slicing/shredding disc make thin slices for parsnip crisps. Mash cooked parsnips by pulsing with the knife blade.

PEARS   Process as for apples.

POTATOES   To chop potatoes use the knife blade; chop coarsely for soup bases or finely for röstis. Be sure to wash potatoes well after chopping or the starch will make them go grey.
    Mash cooked potatoes with butter, milk and seasoning by pulsing with the knife blade. Be careful not to overprocess or the potato will go runny.
    For chips use the standard chipper disc.

For fine chips use the 'Julienne-style' chipper disc.
    For thin rounds for gratins or crisps, peel and cut potatoes to fit the feed tube. Use the pusher to push down onto the slicing shredding disc.
    Or grate coarsely or finely for röstis.

RADISHES   Remove the tops and cut in half. Use the thin slicing/fine shredding disc to slice into circles or grate finely.

SWEDES   To chop coarsely use the knife blade. Mash cooked swedes by pulsing with the knife blade.

TOMATOES   Skin tomatoes by dropping them into boiling water for 10–20 seconds and then popping them out of their skins. Quarter and seed the skinned tomatoes before chopping with the knife blade – coarsely for salsas and finely for sauces and soups.

TURNIPS   Prepare and process as for swedes.

basic recipes

This chapter covers recipes which are easily made in the Kenwood Food Processor and form the basis of hundreds of different dishes. They are, if you like, the staples of food processor cooking.

There is shortcrust pastry that you can use to make savoury or sweet tarts, such as the tasty Courgette, Cheddar and Dijon Tart on page 27, little pasties for picnics like the Spanish Empanadas on page 44, or the classic Pear and Almond Tarts featured on page 48. Next is choux pastry for the naughty-but-nice éclairs and profiteroles – always great for parties whether you're filling them with cream cheese and herbs or smoked fish or sweet creams; they are all easily whipped up in the Kenwood.

There's also a recipe for a basic Victoria Sponge Cake that can be flavoured with a multitude of icings and fillings. Then there's a basic white bread, a delicious loaf that is light and airy. Last of the flour basics is a quick batter that requires no resting time; use it to make pancakes, Yorkshire puddings, fritters or any of their endless variations.

Finally, there are the savoury sauce basics of hummus and chutney. You'll never need to eat plain food again!

batter

Ⓥ Makes: about 14 pancakes   Preparation time: 5 minutes   Freezing: Not Recommended

This recipe is for pouring batter which is suitable for Yorkshire puddings, toad-in-the-hole and pancakes.

125 g (4½ oz) plain flour
a pinch of salt
300 ml (½ pint) milk
1 egg
15 g (½ oz) butter, melted

1. With the knife blade in place, put the flour and salt into the bowl. Turn the machine on and add the milk and egg through the feed tube. Process until blended using the pulse action.

2. Pour the melted butter down the feed tube and pulse again until thoroughly mixed in. Pour the batter into a measuring jug and use as required.

Variation
To make a coating batter suitable for fritters, follow the method as above but use 150 ml (¼ pint) of milk.

shortcrust pastry

ⓥ Makes: enough for a 23 cm (9-inch) tart or to cover the top and bottom of an 18 cm (7-inch) pie plate
Preparation time: 10 minutes plus 20 minutes chilling time   Cooking time: 25 minutes   Freezing: Recommended
Freeze uncooked pastry in an airtight bag for up to three months. Freeze cooked pastry in an airtight rigid
container for up to six months.

Shortcrust pastry is very easy and quick to make in the Kenwood, the trick being to process for the minimum amount of time and to add the water gradually so the pastry doesn't become too wet. Kenwood actually makes better pastry than you could yourself: your hands are warm, the knife blade is not.

125 g (4½ oz) plain flour
60 g (2 oz) cold butter, cut into small pieces
1 egg yolk
a pinch of salt
1–2 tablespoons iced water

1. Put the flour into the food processor with the knife blade and add the butter. Process for 30 seconds or until the mixture looks like coarse breadcrumbs. Add the egg mixture and pulse to mix. Then add the water one tablespoon at a time and pulse until the mixture looks like it is about to stick together.

2. Turn out the mixture onto a work surface and shape into a flat round with your hands, put it into a plastic bag or wrap in clingfilm and chill in the fridge for 20 minutes.

3. Meanwhile, preheat the oven to Gas Mark 4/180°C/350°F and flour a worksurface ready for rolling.

4. Roll the pastry out to a circle to fit the tin or plate that you are using and transfer, pressing into the edges of the tin or plate. Line the tin or plate with a crumpled piece of greaseproof paper or foil, fill with baking beans and bake for 15 minutes. Remove the baking paper and beans and return to the oven for another 10 minutes or until the bottom turns a light golden brown. The pastry case is now ready for filling. (It may be necessary to cover the edges of the pastry case with foil to stop them burning when it is in the oven for the second time.)

Cook's notes
Uncooked pastry can be made a day in advance and kept, wrapped in clingfilm, in the fridge. The cooked pastry case can be made a day in advance and stored, either wrapped in clingfilm or in a sealed freezer bag, in the fridge. If you store the uncooked pastry in the fridge, remove it 30 minutes before you want to roll it out.

Variation
To make a sweet shortcrust pastry just add 25 g (1 oz) icing sugar to the flour, increase the amount of butter to 90 g (3¼ oz) and add ½ teaspoon vanilla essence. Follow the recipe as above, again adding the iced water gradually and processing the pastry as little as possible.

choux pastry

Makes: 12 to 16 fingers or profiteroles   Preparation time: 10 minutes   Cooking time: 15 minutes
Freezing: Not Recommended

Choux pastry can be used to make éclairs, profiteroles or choux buns, or filled with cream cheese and smoked salmon for tasty party nibbles.

200 ml (7 fl oz) water
75 g (2¾ oz) butter
100 g (3½ oz) plain flour
a pinch of salt
3 eggs

1. Fit the knife blade to the food processor. Heat the water and butter together in a small pan over a gentle heat.

2. Place the flour and salt in the processor bowl. When the butter has melted, bring the mixture to the boil and, with the machine running, pour it onto the flour through the feed tube. Process for a few seconds until just combined.

3. Add the eggs, one at a time, and process each for a very few seconds on a low speed until they are just mixed in and the pastry is shiny and thick. Be careful not to overprocess or the batter will be too runny.

4. Preheat the oven to Gas Mark 6/200°C/400°F. Spoon heaped teaspoons (for profiteroles) on a greased baking sheet or fit a piping bag with a plain 1 cm (½-inch) nozzle and pipe small fingers (for éclairs).

5. Bake for 15 minutes or until golden, light and hollow sounding when tapped. Split each profiterole or finger open using a sharp knife while it is still hot, to dry out the inside. Cool the profiteroles or fingers on a wire cooling rack.

6. When completely cool fill with cream, cream cheese or crème pâtissière. If the pastries are sweet, you could top them with chocolate sauce or icing sugar.

victoria sponge cake

**Ⓥ Makes: one 18 cm (7-inch) round cake   Preparation time: 5 minutes   Cooking time: 30 minutes
Freezing: Recommended for the unfilled sponge, placed in an airtight bag or wrapped in clingfilm**

This light, easy all-in-one cake can be made in 40 minutes with the Kenwood – delicious!

100 g (3½ oz) soft margarine
100 g (3½ oz) caster sugar
100 g (3½ oz) self-raising flour
1 teaspoon baking powder
2 eggs
For the filling:
3 tablespoons strawberry jam
150 ml (¼ pint) double cream, whipped (optional)
1 tablespoon icing or caster sugar, to decorate

1. Preheat the oven to Gas Mark 4/180°C/350°F and grease and line two 18 cm (7-inch) shallow loose-bottomed cake tins.

2. Fit the knife blade. Place all the ingredients for the sponge plus 1 tablespoon of warm water in the bowl and process for 5 seconds. Using a spatula, scrape the mixture into the centre of the bowl and process for a further 5 seconds.

3. Pour the mixture into the prepared tins and bake for 30 minutes or until firm to a light touch and coming away from the edges slightly. If you are unsure whether the cake is cooked, insert a thin skewer into the centre and it should come out clean. Turn out onto a wire cooling rack.

4. When cool, spread the jam and cream (if using) over one of the cakes, top with the other cake and sprinkle with the sugar.

pizza dough

Ⓥ Serves: 4   Preparation time: ½ hour plus approximately 30–60 minutes rising time   Cooking time: 10–15 minutes Freezing: Not Recommended

You can make your own pizza dough at home in less than an hour with this simple recipe.

2 teaspoons active dried yeast
a pinch of sugar
350 g (12 oz) strong plain white bread flour, plus extra for dusting
2 teaspoons olive oil
150 ml (¼ pint) water
½ teaspoon salt

1. Mix the yeast with the sugar and 3 tablespoons of warm water (see Cook's notes) and leave for 10 minutes until frothy. Put the flour in the bowl with the dough tool in position. Add the yeast mixture, oil, water and salt in a steady stream down the feed tube. Process until the dough comes together, then process for a few seconds longer to finish kneading, scraping down the sides if necessary with a spatula.

2. Turn out into a bowl and cover with a piece of oiled clingfilm. Leave to rise in a warm place for at least 30 minutes or until doubled in size.

3. Preheat the oven to Gas Mark 9/240°C/475°F. Turn out the dough on to a floured worksurface. Knead for 1 minute and then leave to rise again for 5 minutes. Roll it out or stretch it with your fingers to a 30 cm (12 inch) circle or divide into 4 and stretch each to a circle measuring 10 cm (4 inches). Place the base or bases on a large floured baking sheet, cover with your chosen toppings and then bake for 10–15 minutes until golden and crisp around the edges.

Cook's notes

For a very simple pizza spread the base with ready-made tomato sauce or passata and sprinkle with some chopped fresh herbs, grated cheese and black pepper.

There are two types of dried yeast: active dried yeast and traditional dried yeast. 2 teaspoons active dried yeast is equivalent to 15 g (½ oz) fresh yeast. If using fresh yeast, mix it with the warm water and add a teaspoon of sugar. Leave in a warm place for 15 minutes or until frothy. Then add the liquid to the flour and salt through the feed tube with the processor running. For traditional dried yeast use 2 teaspoons and follow the method for fresh yeast.

To get the warm water to the right temperature mix 2 parts cold water with 1 part boiling water.

Variations

Experiment using other flours such as wholemeal or rye to add some texture to the dough though you may find that you need to add a little extra water to get the right consistency. For an authentic pizza base try using the '00' flour, which is the Italian extra fine flour used to make pasta and is now available in some supermarkets.

basic white bread

ⓥ Makes: 2 medium-sized loaves   Preparation time: 10 minutes plus 1¼ hours rising time   Cooking time: 30 minutes   Freezing: Recommended in airtight plastic bags for up to 3 months

The time and effort involved in breadmaking may put off even the most proficient and enthusiastic cooks, but with a Kenwood to do the work for you there's no reason why you shouldn't enjoy home-baked bread. It has no additives, it tastes better and it's cheaper.

450 g (1 lb) strong white plain flour
2 teaspoons salt
25 g (1 oz) margarine or butter
2 teaspoons (or a 7 g sachet) fast action dried yeast
300 ml (½ pint) warm water
oil for oiling

1. Fit the knife blade to the food processor and combine the flour, salt and margarine for 30 seconds.

2. Add the dried yeast and pulse to combine. Then with the motor running add the water a little bit at a time until the mixture forms a soft dough. Process for 10 seconds more to finish kneading.

3. Take out the dough, put it into a bowl, cover with an oiled piece of clingfilm or a plastic bag, and leave in a warm place for three quarters of an hour or until doubled in size.

4. Divide the dough into two and knead lightly by hand for a minute. Shape into rounds and place on an oiled baking tray. Make two shallow cuts in the top of the loaves to form crosses. Leave to rise for a further 30 minutes and meanwhile preheat the oven to Gas Mark 7/220°C/425°F. Bake the bread for 25–30 minutes until it is golden brown and sounds hollow when tapped on the bottom. Leave to cool on racks before you eat it.

Cook's notes
2 teaspoons fast action dried yeast is equivalent to 15 g (½ oz) fresh yeast. If using fresh yeast then mix it with the warm water and a teaspoon of sugar and leave in a warm place for 15 minutes or until frothy. Then add the liquid to the flour and salt through the feed tube with the processor running. If using active dried yeast use 2 teaspoons and mix it with the warm water and a teaspoon of sugar. Continue as for fresh yeast.

To get the warm water to the right temperature, mix 2 parts cold water with 1 part boiling water.

hummus

Ⅴ Serves: 6–8   Preparation time: 5 minutes   Freezing: Not Recommended

This Middle Eastern chick-pea dish can be eaten with pitta bread and salad, as a dip or stirred into any number of dishes to add texture and flavour. This is a quick and easy version using canned chick-peas.

2 × 400 g (14 oz) cans chick-peas, rinsed and drained
2 tablespoons tahini
1 garlic clove
juice of 1–2 lemons
1 teaspoon salt
pepper

1. With the knife blade fitted and the machine running at top speed, drop in the garlic through the feed tube and process until chopped.

2. Put the remaining ingredients in the bowl with 2 tablespoons of water. Process to a smooth paste, adding more water if required. Taste then adjust the seasoning. Store in the fridge for up to four days.

Cook's note
Tahini is a paste made from ground sesame seeds. It separates during storage, so before use stir well to blend the sesame oil back into the sesame pulp.

spicy tomato chutney

**Ⓥ Makes: about 600 g (1 lb 5 oz)   Preparation time: 10 minutes   Cooking time: 1 hour
Freezing: Not Recommended**

This delicious chutney can be whizzed up in minutes in the Kenwood then eaten fresh with cold meats and cheese, or on sandwiches or baked potatoes. Or store in jars and keep for later in the year when the flavours will have matured. Dessert and cooking apples are equally good in this recipe.

225 g (8 oz) onions, quartered
2 tablespoons olive oil
500 g (1 lb 2 oz) tomatoes
225 g (8 oz) apples, cored
5 cm (2-inch) piece of fresh root ginger, peeled and roughly chopped
1 fresh red or green chilli, de-seeded
1 teaspoon salt
300 ml (½ pint) cider vinegar
1 teaspoon coriander seeds, ground (use the glass multi-mill or a pestle and mortar)
1 teaspoon cumin seeds, ground (as above)
2 tablespoons black treacle
125 g (4½ oz) brown sugar
salt and pepper

1. Fit the thin slicing/fine shredding disc to the bowl and use to slice the onions. Heat the olive oil in a large saucepan and fry the onions until softened, about 5 minutes.

2. Meanwhile, fit the knife blade to the processor and roughly chop the tomatoes, apples, ginger and chilli. Add to the saucepan.

3. Add the remaining ingredients to the pan, bring to the boil and then simmer, without a lid, for about 55 minutes, stirring occasionally, until thick.

4. Taste and adjust the seasoning before pouring into clear glass jars. Store for up to three months in a cool, dark place.

soups, salads and snacks

Whether you need a starter for a dinner party or a quick snack this chapter has lots of tasty ideas. There are three soups, including hearty Bean and Rosemary and light and summery Pea and Mint. There's a tasty tart for a lunch or picnic and an unusual bulb fennel salad that you will love for its flavours and crisp freshness. Last, but not least, deliciously simple and spicy Onion Bhajis.

pea and mint soup with crispy parma ham

Serves: 4 Preparation time: 20 minutes Cooking time: 20 minutes Freezing: Not Recommended

A modern take on the classic pea and ham soup, this is a delicious bright green soup, made with fresh peas – it's full of the flavours of summer.

1 tablespoon olive oil
2 onions, chopped finely
2 garlic cloves, peeled and crushed
1 lettuce, sliced
25 g (1 oz) fresh mint
500 g (1 lb 2 oz) fresh or frozen peas, thawed
a pinch of sugar
600 ml (1 pint) chicken or vegetable stock
150 ml (¼ pint) double cream
4 thin slices Parma ham
fresh chives to garnish (optional)
salt and pepper

1. Heat the oil in a saucepan and fry the onion and garlic for 4 minutes or until softened.

2. Add the lettuce, mint, peas, seasoning and sugar to the pan and bring to the boil. Simmer for 2 minutes.

3. Preheat the grill to high and grill the Parma ham until crispy.

4. Blend the soup in the liquidiser or in the bowl fitted with the knife blade. Check the seasoning and stir in the cream. Reheat the soup in a clean saucepan over a low heat. Chop the grilled ham into small pieces. Divide the soup between 4 serving dishes and sprinkle the ham and chives (if using) over.

Cook's note

If you can't find Parma ham then grill 4 rashers of bacon until crispy, chop and sprinkle over the soup instead.

Variation

Substitute the lettuce for 5 large sorrel leaves – its bitterness partners the sweet pea flavour perfectly.

bean and rosemary soup with red pepper purée

**Ⓥ (If using vegetable stock)   Serves: 6   Preparation time: 5 minutes   Cooking time: 15 minutes
Freezing: Not Recommended**

This moreish, hearty soup is based on a traditional Italian recipe using cannellini beans. Serve it with the home-made white bread (page 19) for a warming lunch on a cold day.

For the soup:
1 large carrot
1 large onion
2 garlic cloves
2 tablespoons olive oil
3 × 300 g (10½ oz) cans cannellini beans, rinsed and drained
8 sprigs of rosemary, chopped finely
2 litres (3½ pints) chicken or vegetable stock
salt and pepper
For the purée:
2 red peppers, halved, de-seeded and stalks removed
a pinch of salt

1. Chop the carrot, onion and garlic, using the knife blade. Heat the oil in a large saucepan then gently fry the vegetables until they begin to soften, about 4 minutes.

2. Add the beans, rosemary and stock and bring to the boil. Simmer gently for 10 minutes.

3. Meanwhile make the red pepper purée: grill the peppers skin side up until charred, then put in a plastic bag until cool. When the peppers are cool enough to handle, peel them and put in the bowl with the knife blade, or in the liquidiser. Add a pinch of salt and 2 tablespoons of water to the peppers and purée. Check the seasoning and reserve.

4. Spoon out half the soup from the pan, allow to cool slightly and process until smooth. Return it to the remaining soup in the pan and reheat, stirring. Taste to check the seasoning. Serve the soup with the red pepper purée swirled on top.

roasted tomato soup with basil oil

Ⓥ **Serves: 4**   **Preparation time: 15 minutes**   **Cooking time: 45 minutes**   **Freezing: Not Recommended**

The tomatoes are roasted to intensify their flavour and blended with roast onions and garlic to make a rich, flavoursome soup. Basil oil drizzled over the soup in serving bowls provides a delicious contrast in colour, texture and flavour.

For the soup:

| 4 medium onions, unpeeled and halved |
| 1 bulb garlic, split into cloves and unpeeled |
| 1 kg (2 lb 4 oz) tomatoes, halved |
| 2 tablespoons olive oil |
| 2 tablespoons balsamic vinegar |
| 1 tablespoon sugar |
| salt and pepper |

For the basil oil:

| 15 g (½ oz) fresh basil, washed and dried |
| 8 tablespoons extra virgin olive oil |
| a pinch of salt |

1. Preheat the oven to Gas Mark 6/200°C/400°F. Put the onions, garlic and tomatoes in a roasting tray, add the oil, vinegar, sugar and seasoning and toss together. Roast for 45 minutes or until soft and blackened at the edges.

2. Meanwhile make the basil oil. Put the basil and olive oil in the liquidiser or in the bowl fitted with the knife blade. Process until very smooth. Strain the oil through a fine sieve and pour into a bottle.

3. Remove the vegetables from the oven, allow to cool slightly then peel the onions and garlic. Put the roasted vegetables in the liquidiser with 400 ml (14 fl oz) water and blend until smooth.

4. Pour the soup into a pan and gently heat through, check the seasoning and add more sugar if needed. Pour into 4 serving dishes and serve drizzled with the basil oil.

Cook's note
The basil oil will keep for up to one week in a cool, dark place.

Variations
Fresh coriander and parsley work just as well in this recipe to make the flavoured oil.

courgette, cheddar and dijon tart

Ⓥ Serves: 8 Preparation time: making + chilling pastry + 20 minutes Cooking time: cooking pastry case + 45 minutes Freezing: Not Recommended

With the aid of your Kenwood this tasty tart could not be simpler to prepare. It is just as good served hot or cold.

1 quantity shortcrust pastry (page 14)
275 g (9½ oz) courgettes, tops removed
2 tablespoons olive oil
2 garlic cloves, peeled and crushed
2 eggs
1 egg yolk
300 ml (½ pint) double cream or crème fraîche
1–2 tablespoons Dijon mustard
175 g (6 oz) Cheddar cheese
salt and pepper

1. Roll out the pastry to fit a 23 cm (9-inch) round flat tin and bake blind (see step 4, page 14).

2. Slice the courgettes in the bowl. Heat the oil in a large frying pan and fry the garlic for 1 minute, then add the courgettes and stir-fry over a high heat for 4 minutes.

3. Preheat the oven to Gas Mark 4/180°C/350°F. Grate the cheese using a shredding disc and put in a large bowl. Add the eggs, egg yolk, cream, mustard and the seasoning and beat together.

4. Put the courgettes into the tart case and then pour in half the egg mixture. Place the tart on a baking tray, place on the oven shelf and pour in the remaining egg mixture. Bake for 30–40 minutes until the filling is set but not too firm.

fennel and parmesan salad

Ⓥ **Serves: 4** **Preparation time: 10 minutes** **Freezing: Not Recommended**

This salad is made using bulb fennel – a very popular vegetable in Italy. It combines the aniseed crispness of the fennel and the rich tang of parmesan with a hint of garlic and lemon.

2 fennel bulbs
200 g (7 oz) parmesan cheese
1 garlic clove, crushed
juice of 1 lemon
4 tablespoons extra virgin olive oil
salt and pepper

1. Slice the fennel into pieces that will fit into the feed tube and then using the fine 'Julienne-style' chipper disc, slice into batons. Place the fennel in a serving dish. Grate the parmesan cheese with the fine shredding disc and add to the fennel.

2. Add the remaining ingredients to the dish, stir well and taste to check the seasoning. Add more lemon or salt if required and serve.

Cook's note
This salad can be made up to an hour in advance and left to marinate but check the seasoning just before serving.

onion bhajis with cucumber raita

(V) **Makes: up to 50 cocktail-sized bhajis or 25 larger ones**   **Preparation time: 15 minutes**
Cooking time: 30 minutes (3 batches of bhajis at 10 minutes each)   **Freezing: Recommended**

These popular Indian snacks are really easy to make – it's the cooking that takes the time. Chick-pea (also known as besan, gram or channa) flour is used in this recipe and can be bought from most Asian stores. If you can't find it substitute with ordinary white flour. Serve these tasty bhajis with the cooling cucumber raita or a selection of chutneys.

4 large onions, cut to fit the feed tube
225 g (8 oz) chick-pea flour or plain white flour
2 teaspoons ground cumin
2 teaspoons ground coriander seeds
½ teaspoon turmeric
1 teaspoon chilli powder
2 teaspoons salt
150 ml (¼ pint) water
a small bunch of fresh coriander, chopped
1 litre (1¾ pints) vegetable oil for deep frying
For the raita:
½ cucumber
250 g (9 oz) natural yogurt
a bunch of fresh mint, chopped
a pinch of salt

1. Put the onions in the bowl fitted with the knife blade. Chop and then transfer to a large bowl. In the processor bowl put the flour, spices, salt and water; blend to a smooth paste. Place in the bowl with the onions, add the coriander and mix well.

2. Heat the oil in a wok or deep fat fryer to 190°C/375°F or until it begins to smoke. A drop of the mixture will immediately rise to the surface and brown when it is at the right temperature. If you're using a wok, then reduce the heat to low in order to maintain the right temperature. If you're using an electric fryer it will maintain the temperature by itself.

3. Using either 2 teaspoons for cocktail-sized bhajis, or 2 dessertspoons for larger ones, scoop spoonfuls of the onion mixture into the oil. Use the second spoon to push the mixture off the first.

4. Fry a few bhajis at a time, turning them occasionally. When they are dark brown, after about 10 minutes, take them out with a slotted spoon and drain on kitchen paper. Put them on a plate in a warm oven while you fry the others.

5. To make the raita, grate the cucumber and mix into the yogurt with the mint and salt.

meat and
poultry

This is a truly international chapter bringing you easy-to-prepare recipes from all over the world. Use the Kenwood to make the marinade and sauce for Chicken Satays with Peanut Satay Sauce and to prepare Mexican Tortillas and an easy all-in-one guacamole. Fragrant Lamb Koftas are served with Green Herb Salsa while French Escalopes of Pork are accompanied with a deliciously sticky onion confit that takes just seconds to prepare in the Kenwood.

escalopes of pork with onion confit

Serves: 4   Preparation time: 15 minutes   Cooking time: 40 minutes   Freezing: Not Recommended

Onion confit (a caramelised onion relish) can be made in advance and kept, covered, in the fridge for 2 weeks.

For the onion confit:

1 kg (2 lb 4 oz) onions

2 tablespoons olive oil

2 tablespoons red wine vinegar

4 tablespoons caster sugar

For the pork:

4 pork escalopes

75 g (2¾ oz) bread

a small bunch of fresh parsley

25 g (1 oz) flour

2 eggs, beaten

2 tablespoons olive oil

salt and pepper

1. Slice the onions with the thinnest slicing disc. Heat the oil in a large frying pan then add the onions, vinegar and sugar. Stir to mix well then cook gently over a low heat, stirring occasionally for 35 minutes. Spoon into a jar or bowl and store in the fridge until ready to use.

2. Place the pork between two sheets of greaseproof paper, foil or clingfilm and pound with a rolling pin or meat tenderiser until thin.

3. Place the bread and the parsley in the bowl with the knife blade fitted and process to fine breadcrumbs. Tip out onto a large plate. Put the flour on another plate and season. Dip each escalope in the flour, then in the egg and finally cover with breadcrumbs.

4. Heat the oil in a frying pan and fry the breaded pork for 2–3 minutes on each side, until golden and cooked through. Serve with the confit and new potatoes or mash.

Cook's note

The onion confit is also delicious served with cold meats and cheese.

mexican tortillas with spicy beef and guacamole

Serves: 4 **Preparation time: 25 minutes** **Cooking time: 25 minutes** **Freezing: Not Recommended**

Make the dough for these tortillas in the Kenwood, fill with spicy beef and home-made guacamole, and serve with lashings of soured cream – fantastic!

For the spicy beef:

2 onions

2 garlic cloves

1 tablespoon olive oil

400 g (14 oz) minced beef

400 g (14 oz) can of chopped tomatoes

2 small chillies, de-seeded and chopped finely

1 tablespoon of Worcestershire sauce

a pinch of sugar

salt and pepper

For the tortillas:

250 g (9 oz) plain flour

200 g (7 oz) rye flour

2 teaspoons groundnut oil

2 teaspoons salt

250 ml (9 fl oz) water

For the guacamole:

2 avocados, peeled and stoned

1 garlic clove

½ red onion

1 tomato

juice of 1 lemon

salt and pepper

To serve:

lettuce, tomato salsa and soured cream

1. Chop the onion and garlic. Heat the oil in a saucepan and fry the onion and garlic for 4 minutes. Add the beef and stir until browned all over. Add the chopped tomatoes, chillies, Worcestershire sauce, sugar and seasoning. Bring to the boil and then simmer for 20 minutes.

2. Meanwhile put all the tortilla ingredients into the bowl fitted with the knife blade. Process to form a smooth dough, adding a little more water if necessary.

3. Turn out the dough on a floured work surface and cut into 12 pieces. Shape each piece into a ball and then flatten slightly. Roll each ball into a circle measuring about 20 cm (8 inches) in diameter.

4. Heat a griddle or frying pan and dry-fry each tortilla until the surface becomes bubbly. Turn over with tongs and press down the edges with a fish slice. As soon as brown spots begin to appear on the underside the tortilla is ready (about 6 minutes cooking in all). Keep warm, wrapped in a tea towel or foil, in a warm oven whilst you cook the others.

5. For the guacamole, put all the ingredients in the bowl fitted with the knife blade. Pulse to form a coarse paste. Taste and season, adding more lemon juice if necessary. Put in a bowl in the fridge.

6. To serve, place a large spoonful of meat and some guacamole on each tortilla and roll up, serve with shredded lettuce, tomato salsa and sour cream.

Cook's notes
Rye flour is available in health food shops or some supermarkets. Beef can be minced in the bowl with the knife blade.

lamb kofta on green herb salsa

Serves: 4   Preparation time: 20 minutes + 1 hour chilling   Cooking time: 8 minutes   Freezing Recommended uncooked only; thaw completely before cooking

These fragrant kebabs are popular street food in Morocco, Tunisia and Algeria, served in warmed pitta bread with a sprinkling of salt and cumin. They are also delicious with tsatsíki and hummus.

For the kebabs:

50 g (1¾ oz) bread

400 g (14 oz) minced lamb

1 egg, beaten lightly

a small bunch of fresh parsley

1 onion

½ teaspoon ground allspice

¼ teaspoon cayenne pepper

1 teaspoon ground cumin

1 teaspoon paprika

1 tablespoon olive oil

salt and pepper

For the salsa:

a bunch of fresh parsley

a bunch of fresh coriander

4 spring onions

2 tablespoons olive oil

4 tomatoes, quartered and de-seeded

4 tablespoons green or black olives

2 tablespoons capers

a pinch of sugar

zest and juice of 1 lemon

salt and pepper

pitta bread, to serve

oil for brushing

8 wooden skewers soaked in water or 8 metal skewers

1. To make the kebabs, fit the knife blade to the bowl. Add the bread and process to make fine breadcrumbs. Add all the other ingredients and mix to a paste.

2. With moistened hands, take generous tablespoons of the paste and mould into 10 cm (4-inch) long finger shapes around the skewers. Put on a tray then refrigerate for 1 hour.

3. Meanwhile make the herb salsa, put all the ingredients in the clean food processor bowl and chop to a coarse paste. Turn out into a serving bowl and refrigerate.

4. Preheat the grill and cover the grill pan with foil. Brush the foil with a little oil then put the skewers onto it and grill for 4 minutes on each side. To serve, slide the kebabs off the skewers into warmed pitta bread and spoon in the salsa.

chicken satays with peanut satay sauce

Ⓥ **Serves: 4** **Preparation time: 30 minutes chilling time + 15 minutes** **Cooking time: 10 minutes**
Freezing: Not Recommended

Tender strips of chicken breast marinated in garlic, ginger and soy, and then grilled and served with a peanut, coconut and lime sauce.

4 chicken breasts, sliced into long strips
20 wooden skewers, soaked in water
For the marinade:
2 cloves garlic, peeled
2.5 cm (1-inch) piece of fresh root ginger, peeled
2 tablespoons light soy sauce
1 tablespoon honey
For the satay sauce:
200 g (7 oz) roasted peanuts or 4 tablespoons crunchy peanut butter
½ teaspoon chilli powder
juice of 1 lime
100 ml (3½ fl oz) coconut milk
salt to taste

1. Fit the knife blade in the bowl and add the marinade ingredients, and blend until smooth. Place the chicken in a bowl and pour over the marinade. Leave for at least 30 minutes in the fridge.

2. Preheat the grill to high. Thread the chicken onto the skewers and grill for 3 minutes on each side or until golden brown and cooked through.

3. Put all the sauce ingredients in the bowl (there is no need to wash it from the marinade) and blend until smooth. Check the seasoning and add more salt or lime juice if necessary. Put in a bowl and serve with the grilled chicken.

Cook's note
Satays are ideal for cooking on a barbecue.

Variations
Try using prawns or pork fillet instead of the chicken.

fish and shellfish

This chapter is full of new flavours and textures for you to try. There are little Thai Fish Cakes, dipped into a fiery, hot and sweet sauce and served as a starter or main course. Then there is the Crab and Noodle Salad dressed with a fresh mango vinaigrette that is whizzed up in no time in the Kenwood. Lastly, there are Fish Goujons, covered in a crispy, nutty coating and served with a moreish avocado dip.

thai fish cakes with sweet and hot dip

Serves: 4   Preparation time: 10 minutes + chilling time   Cooking time: 20 minutes   Freezing: Not Recommended

These little fish cakes are quite different to the traditional British type – light and spicy.

For the fish cakes:

300 g (10½ oz) fish fillets e.g. cod, haddock or salmon, chopped roughly

100 g (3½ oz) frozen prawns, thawed

1 tablespoon red curry paste (see Cook's notes)

2 kaffir lime leaves, finely chopped (optional)

a small bunch of fresh coriander

1 teaspoon salt

100 g (3½ oz) green beans, chopped finely

2 tablespoons groundnut oil for frying

For the dipping sauce:

2 small cucumbers, quartered lengthways

1 small red or green chilli, de-seeded and sliced finely

1½ teaspoons sugar

3 tablespoons rice or white wine vinegar

1 tablespoon roasted peanuts

fresh coriander leaves, to garnish

1. Put the fish, prawns, curry paste, lime leaves, coriander and salt in the bowl with the knife blade and process to a fine paste, then add the beans and pulse to mix in. Turn out of the processor and place in a bowl. Refrigerate the mixture for up to 1 hour.

2. Meanwhile make the dipping sauce. Slice the cucumber in the food processor and put into a bowl with the chilli. Combine the sugar, vinegar and 1 tablespoon of water in a saucepan and heat until the sugar has dissolved. Cool and pour over the cucumber. Spoon into little dipping bowls. Clean the bowl and then chop the peanuts roughly. Sprinkle on top with the coriander leaves.

3. With greased hands, shape tablespoons of the fish mixture into small patties. Heat the oil in a frying pan and fry the cakes for 10 minutes on each side until golden and cooked through. Lift out with a fish slice and drain on kitchen paper. Serve the fish cakes with the dipping sauce.

Cook's notes

You can make your own red curry paste in the multi-mill, mini-processor bowl or liquidiser. Simply blend the following ingredients together until smooth: 2 large red chillies (de-seeded), 1 stalk lemongrass (peeled), 2.5 cm (1-inch) piece fresh root ginger (peeled), a large handful of fresh coriander, the juice and zest of 1 lime (preferably a Kaffir), 4 garlic cloves, 4 shallots, 1 tablespoon of fish sauce and 1 teaspoon each of salt and sugar. The paste will keep in the fridge for up to one week.

crab and noodle salad with mango dressing

Serves: 4   Preparation time: 15 minutes   Cooking time: 3–4 minutes   Freezing: Not Recommended

This Oriental-style salad makes a substantial lunch or supper dish – with the refreshing mango dressing it is ideal to serve on a hot summer's day.

For the salad:

4 celery sticks

6 spring onions

1 red onion, halved

2 small red chillies, de-seeded

100 g (3½ oz) mange-tout, trimmed

200 g (7 oz) carrots, peeled

125 g (4½ oz) roasted peanuts

a bunch of fresh coriander

350 g (12 oz) fresh crabmeat or 2 × 170 g (6 oz) cans of crab, drained

200 g (7 oz) noodles (see Cook's note)

For the dressing:

1 mango, peeled and stoned

juice of 1 lime

salt and pepper

1. Fit the thin slicing/fine shredding disc to the bowl. Slice all the vegetables and place them in a large serving bowl. With the knife blade in the processor, pulse the peanuts and coriander to roughly chop and add to the vegetables with the crab.

2. Cook the noodles according to the packet instructions, drain and refresh with cold water. Add to the vegetables and crab and stir well.

3. Make the dressing. Put the mango in the processor with the knife blade, or in the liquidiser, add the lime juice and one or two tablespoons of water and purée to a smooth dressing. Taste to check the seasoning then pour over the salad and toss lightly together. Serve immediately.

Cook's note

You can use any kind of noodle for this salad from glass noodles, rice vermicelli to buckwheat or egg noodles.

Variation

Instead of the mango vinaigrette this salad could be dressed with soy sauce and lime juice.

nut-crusted fish goujons with avocado dip

Serves: 4   Preparation time: 15 minutes   Cooking time: 12 minutes   Freezing: Not Recommended

These little fingers of fish are coated in a crispy nut crumb and fried, then served with a creamy avocado dip.

For the goujons:

4 thick slices bread
2 tablespoons walnuts, hazelnuts or cashew nuts, toasted
25 g (1 oz) plain flour
8 × 150 g (5½ oz) fillets plaice or lemon sole, skinned and sliced into thick strips
2 eggs, beaten
2 tablespoons groundnut oil
1 teaspoon sesame oil
salt and pepper

For the avocado dressing:

2 ripe avocados
1 garlic clove
225 g (8 oz) natural Greek yogurt
2–3 sprigs fresh dill, roughly chopped

1. Fit the knife blade to the bowl. Finely chop the bread and nuts to form crumbs, then tip out onto a plate. Put the flour on a plate and season. Dip the fish first in the flour to coat, then in the beaten egg and lastly in the nut crumb mix.

2. Meanwhile make the avocado dip. Place all the dressing ingredients in the bowl with the knife blade. Whizz until smooth. Check the seasoning and place in a serving bowl.

3. Heat the oils in a frying pan and fry the crumbed fish for 3 minutes on each side until golden and cooked through. Remove from the pan with a fish slice and drain on kitchen paper before serving hot with the dip.

vegetables

Whether you are a vegetarian or need an accompaniment to a main meal this chapter has some tasty ideas. There's the rich and creamy Jansson's Temptation, a potato gratin with caramelised onions, and a healthy Thai-style Vegetable Omelette, full of vegetables chopped the no-fuss way in the Kenwood. Also, Spanish Empanadas which are a bit like Cornish pasties – light and flaky with a fresh, spicy vegetable filling. Lastly there's the Potato Rösti Florentine which can be made up quickly and easily for a breakfast to beat all others, or a light lunch or supper.

jansson's temptation

Serves: 4   Preparation time: 15 minutes   Cooking time: 40 minutes   Freezing: Not Recommended

This is a classic Swedish gratin of finely shredded potato, anchovies and onions baked in cream. It's temptation indeed though no-one seems to know who Jansson was!

1 kg (2 lb 4 oz) potatoes, preferably waxy ones like Désirée
2 large onions, peeled and cut in half to fit down the feed tube
50 g (1¾ oz) butter
100 g (3½ oz) can of anchovy fillets, washed
300 ml (½ pint) single cream
150 ml (¼ pint) milk
salt and pepper

1. Grate the potatoes then put them in a colander. Then grate the onions.

2. Grease a large (about 25 cm × 30 cm/10-inch × 12-inch) gratin dish with a little butter. Melt half the remaining butter in a pan and add the onions. Cook for 10 minutes until golden and soft.

3. Wash the potatoes and dry them in a tea towel. Layer some potatoes, then a few onions, then a few anchovies in the gratin dish. Repeat the layers finishing with a layer of potatoes and seasoning between each layer.

4. Preheat the oven to Gas Mark 5/190°C/375°F. Dot the potatoes with the remaining butter and pour over the cream and milk. Bake for 40 minutes or until the potatoes are tender and golden.

Variation

For a vegetarian version, omit the anchovies and add 1 red pepper, chopped finely in between the potato and onion layers.

stir-fry vegetable omelettes

Serves: 2   Preparation time: 10 minutes   Cooking time: 10 minutes   Freezing: Not Recommended

Stir-fried beansprouts, shredded carrot, mushrooms and baby sweetcorn parcelled in a Thai-style omelette – delicious!

For the filling:

2 garlic cloves

4 spring onions

100 g (3½ oz) baby sweetcorns

100 g (3½ oz) mushrooms

100 g (3½ oz) carrots, peeled

2 tablespoons peanut oil

100 g (3½ oz) beansprouts

1 tablespoon light soy sauce

1½ teaspoons sugar

For the omelettes:

4 eggs

1 teaspoon fish sauce

½ teaspoon sugar

salt and pepper

1 tablespoon peanut oil

chives, to garnish (optional)

1. First make the filling. Fit the thin slicing disc to the bowl. Slice the garlic, then spring onions, baby sweetcorn, mushrooms and carrots.

2. Heat the oil in a large frying pan or wok and stir-fry the chopped vegetables, beansprouts, soy sauce and sugar over a high heat for 5 minutes or until just cooked but still crunchy. Turn out onto a plate and keep warm.

3. Beat together the eggs, fish sauce, sugar and seasoning. Heat half of the oil in the frying pan or wok, swirl around to completely cover, then pour in half of the egg mixture and swirl around to thinly coat the pan. When the egg is cooked put half the filling in the centre and, using a palette knife, roll the omelette over it and then slide it onto a plate.

4. Keep warm while you repeat the procedure with the remaining egg mixture. Serve garnished with chives, if using.

potato rösti florentine

V **Serves: 4   Preparation time: 30 minutes   Cooking time: 30 minutes   Freezing: Not Recommended**

Potato rösti is always popular; here it is served with poached eggs and spinach with a creamy hollandaise sauce.

For the rösti:

900 g (2 lb) waxy potatoes (i.e. Desirée), peeled

½ teaspoon cayenne pepper

2 tablespoons olive oil

salt and pepper

For the eggs and spinach:

200 g (7 oz) spinach, washed and thick stems removed

a pinch of freshly grated nutmeg

25 g (1 oz) butter

1 teaspoon vinegar

4 eggs

salt and pepper

For the Hollandaise sauce:

4 egg yolks

1 tablespoon lemon juice

¼ teaspoon salt

225 g (8 oz) butter

1. Put the potatoes in a pan and cover with hot water. Bring to the boil and boil for 5 minutes then drain. Fit the coarse shredding disc to the bowl and shred the potatoes. Put in a bowl and add the cayenne and seasoning. Mix well.

2. Heat the oil in a frying pan. Take 8 handfuls of the potato mixture and squeeze together before putting them into the pan. Press down the mounds with a fish slice but be careful to keep them as rounds. Turn down the heat and leave to brown for at least 10 minutes. Then carefully turn over and leave to brown again. Lift out with the fish slice and drain on kitchen paper. Place two on each serving plate and keep warm.

3. Meanwhile put the spinach in a pan with the nutmeg, butter and seasoning. Cover and cook over a low heat for 5 minutes, until wilted. Stir together.

4. To make the Hollandaise, fit the knife blade to the bowl and add the eggs, lemon juice and salt. Melt the butter but do not let it become too hot. Run the machine to mix the eggs, then pour in the butter in a constant stream through the feed tube with the machine running. The sauce should be smooth and shiny. Check the seasoning.

5. Put a pan of water on to boil and add the vinegar. Break the eggs into a ramekin or small bowl one by one. Then gently tip each one into the boiling water. Remove after 2 minutes with a slotted spoon.

6. To serve, top the rösti with some spinach and an egg. Pour over a little hollandaise sauce and serve immediately.

spanish empanadas

**Ⓥ Makes: 12 (serve at least 3 for a main course, 2 for a starter)   Preparation time: making + chilling pastry +
15 minutes   Cooking time: 2 batches at 3–5 minutes each   Freezing: Not Recommended**

Empanadas are traditional deep-fried pastry turnovers filled with a savoury or sweet filling. These veggie versions are filled with goat's cheese and a mixture of spicy vegetables. Serve with the Spicy Tomato Chutney (page 21).

1 quantity shortcrust pastry (page 14)
For the filling:
1 onion
2 celery sticks
2 carrots, peeled and halved lengthways
½ Savoy cabbage, cut into pieces
2 tablespoons olive oil
50 g (1¾ oz) goat's cheese, crumbled
½ teaspoon paprika
salt and pepper

1. Fit the thin slicing disc to the bowl and slice the vegetables. Heat the oil in a large frying pan and fry the vegetables, with the lid on, for 10 minutes, stirring occasionally.

2. Turn off the heat and mix in the cheese, paprika and seasoning.

3. Roll out the pastry to about 5 mm (¼ inch) thick and then cut out twelve 10 cm (4-inch) rounds. Put one tablespoon of filling in each, a little off centre so that you can then fold the pastry over to make a pasty shape. Seal by pressing the edges together with the prongs of a fork.

4. Heat the oil in a deep pan or deep fat fryer to 190°C/375°F.

5. Fry the empanadas in batches, turning once, for 3–5 minutes until golden brown and cooked through. Drain on kitchen paper and serve.

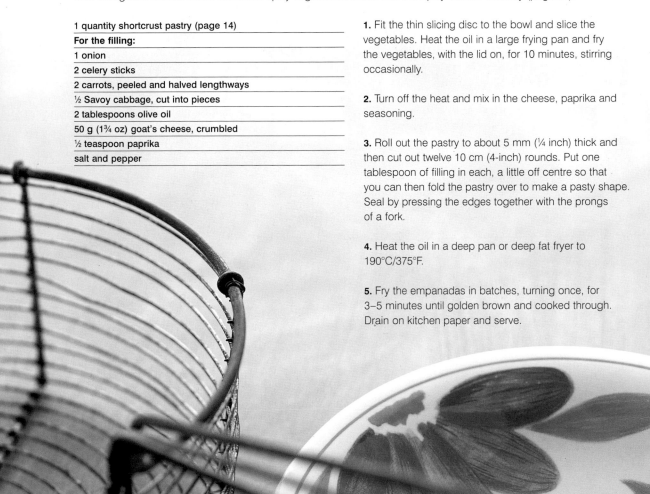

cakes and
desserts

This chapter is a very brief introduction to the hundreds of different desserts, cakes and biscuits you can whizz up in your Kenwood, ranging from homely family cakes to sophisticated dinner-party desserts. You'll find all the cakes a doddle to make and there are some super-quick recipes, like the Peach Melba Fool, which are ideal for midweek. The sumptuous Cookies and Cream Ice Cream rivals even the best ice creams in the shops and takes only minutes to make. The recipe includes a vanilla custard that, of course, you could use on its own to accompany other desserts.

cookies and cream ice cream

V **Serves: 6–8** **Preparation time: 20 minutes plus 3 hours freezing** **Cooking time: 20 minutes**
Freezing: Recommended

The tastiest creamy vanilla ice cream made with ease in the Kenwood then stirred through with crunchy cookies.

4 egg yolks

100 g (3½ oz) caster sugar

300 ml (½ pint) single cream

1 vanilla pod, halved lengthways

1 teaspoon vanilla essence

100 g (3½ oz) Bourbon/Oreo or other chocolate biscuits

300 ml (½ pint) double cream

1. Fit the knife blade to the processor then blend the yolks and sugar together until thick and pale, about 3 minutes.

2. Scrape the seeds from the vanilla pod into a small pan, add the single cream and vanilla essence and heat. When the cream is just below boiling point, and with the machine running, pour the cream in a constant stream into the egg mixture through the feed tube. Blend for a few seconds.

3. Transfer the custard into a clean saucepan and heat gently, stirring all the time, until the sauce begins to thicken. This will take about 10 minutes. Then leave to cool.

4. Fit the knife blade to the processor and chop the biscuits roughly. Stir into the custard mixture.

5. Whip the double cream in the food processor until it forms soft peaks (this happens very quickly – in under a minute – so be careful not to over-whip). Fold the cream into the custard.

6. Pour into a freezer container with a lid and freeze for 1 hour. Remove and stir well, then freeze again, for at least 2 hours, until hard.

7. Remove the ice cream from the freezer 30 minutes before you want to serve it to allow it to soften slightly.

Variations
There are any number of variations for this recipe, just add whatever flavourings you fancy to the mixture, such as 100 g (3½ oz) melted chocolate, 3 tablespoons strong coffee, 200 g (7 oz) puréed fresh strawberries, raspberries or mangoes, as you fold in the cream.

pear and almond tarts

Ⓥ **Serves: 4** **Preparation time: 30 minutes making + chilling pastry + 10 minutes**
Cooking time: cooking pastry cases + 40–55 minutes **Freezing: Recommended**

This delicious tart can be made in one large pastry case or four individual ones, each with half a pear – ideal for picnics or packed lunches and sure to be a popular choice.

1 quantity shortcrust pastry (page 14)
2 ripe pears, peeled, halved and cored
For the almond frangipane:
125 g (4½ oz) caster sugar
125 g (4½ oz) unsalted butter
1 teaspoon almond essence
2 drops of vanilla essence
2 eggs
2 egg yolks
125 g (4½ oz) ground almonds
2 tablespoons plain flour

1. Roll out the pastry to fit a 23 cm (9-inch) round flan tin or four 12 cm (4½-inch) tins and bake blind (see step 4, page 14).

2. Fit the knife blade to the bowl and cream together the sugar, butter and almond and vanilla essence until pale and fluffy. Then add the eggs and yolks, one by one, mixing each one in thoroughly.

3. Add the ground almonds and sieve in the flour, then pulse until just mixed in.

4. Preheat the oven to Gas Mark 3/170°C/320°F. Place the pear halves in the large case or one half in each individual tart. Pour over the frangipane. Bake the large tart for 55 minutes or the individual tarts for 40 minutes or until golden brown.

peach melba fool

ⓥ Serves: 4   Preparation time: 2 minutes   Freezing: Not Recommended

This is a super-quick and easy refreshing summer dessert.

4 ripe peaches, peeled or 400 g (14 oz) can of peaches, drained
300 g (10½ oz) raspberries, fresh or frozen and thawed
1–2 tablespoons icing sugar
300 ml (½ pint) whipping cream
1–2 crumbled meringues, amaretti biscuits or macaroons (optional)

1. With the knife blade fitted to the bowl, purée the peaches, raspberries and icing sugar together, then pour into a serving bowl.

2. Fit the whisk attachment and whisk the cream until it is just holding soft peaks. Fold the cream through the fruit purée with the meringues or biscuits, if using.

Variations
Most soft fruits can be used for this recipe – try mangoes, kiwis, blackberries, strawberries or blueberries or a combination of fruit.

For a healthier version use low-fat fromage frais instead of the cream.

banana cake with coconut cream

V **Serves: 12   Preparation time: 15 minutes   Cooking time: 1 hour   Freezing: Not Recommended**

This cake is made from start to finish in the Kenwood and looks and tastes fantastic!

For the coconut cream:

100 g (3½ oz) creamed coconut

400 g (14 oz) crème fraîche

2 tablespoons icing sugar

For the banana cake:

5 large bananas

125 g (4½ oz) butter, softened

125 g (4½ oz) pecan nuts

350 g (12 oz) self-raising flour

½ teaspoon bicarbonate of soda

250 g (9 oz) light muscovado sugar

3 large eggs

1 fresh coconut, to make toasted coconut shavings (optional)

1. Preheat the oven to Gas Mark 4/180°C/350°F. Grease and line a 20 cm (8-inch) loose-bottomed cake tin.

2. Make the coconut cream by dissolving the creamed coconut in 3 tablespoons of hot water then folding in the crème fraîche and the icing sugar. Chill until the cake is ready.

3. To make the cake, fit the knife blade into the bowl. Add the bananas and process until mashed. Add all the remaining cake ingredients except the pecans and process until well combined. Add the pecans and pulse until just roughly chopped in the mixture.

4. Pour the cake mix into the prepared tin and bake for 1 hour or until a skewer inserted into the middle of the cake comes out clean. Allow the cake to cool completely in the tin.

5. When cool remove from the tin, peel off the lining paper and transfer to a serving plate. Spoon the coconut cream over the top and sides and spread to cover.

6. Make coconut shavings by removing the flesh from the coconut and peeling thin strips using a potato peeler. Toast them under the grill for a few minutes until golden. Cool, then sprinkle on the cake before serving.

lemon polenta cake

Ⓥ **Serves: 10**   **Preparation time: 10 minutes**   **Cooking time: 30 minutes**   **Freezing: Recommended**

A moist, tangy cake which oozes lemon flavour. The polenta not only gives it a sunny yellow colour but also an interesting texture. Serve the cake with fresh strawberries or raspberries and cream.

125 g (4½ oz) butter
115 g (4 oz) polenta (ordinary or quick-cook)
115 g (4 oz) self-raising flour
2 eggs
175 g (6 oz) caster sugar
grated zest and juice of 2 lemons
150 ml (¼ pint) soured cream or natural yogurt
icing sugar to dust (optional)

1. Preheat the oven to Gas Mark 4/180°C/350°F. Grease and line a 20 cm (8-inch) loose-bottomed cake tin.

2. Fit the knife blade to the bowl. Place the butter, polenta and flour in the bowl and process for 30 seconds until the mixture resembles fine breadcrumbs. Add the eggs, one at a time, with the processor still running.

3. Turn off the machine and add the sugar, lemon rind and juice and soured cream or yogurt. Pulse to mix in thoroughly. Spoon the mixture into the prepared tin, smooth the top and bake for 30 minutes or until a metal skewer inserted into the middle comes out clean.

4. Turn out onto a cooling rack and dust with icing sugar (if using) to serve.

strawberry shortcakes

**Ⓥ Makes: about 25 biscuits   Preparation time: 10 minutes   Cooking time: 10 minutes   Freezing: Recommended
The uncooked dough can be frozen for up to 3 months**

These melt-in-your-mouth shortcakes are so simple to prepare in the Kenwood. They can be on the table in 20 minutes from start to finish – a lovely treat for afternoon tea.

175 g (6 oz) unsalted butter
75 g (2¾ oz) caster sugar
2 drops of vanilla essence
grated zest of 1 lemon
225 g (8 oz) plain flour, sieved
caster sugar for dusting
strawberries and whipped cream, to serve

1. Preheat the oven to Gas Mark 4/180°C/350°F and grease and line 2 large greaseproof sheets with baking paper.

2. Fit the knife blade to the bowl and cream the butter, sugar and vanilla essence together for a few minutes until pale and fluffy. Then add the lemon zest and the plain flour. Process to a soft dough, scraping down the sides and bottom of the bowl once or twice with a spatula.

3. Lightly flour a worksurface and tip the dough out onto it. Pat together lightly with your hands and sprinkle with a little flour. Roll out to 5 mm (¼-inch) thickness using a little more flour if the dough sticks. Cut out the biscuits using a pastry cutter and place them on the baking sheets, leaving plenty of space around each one to allow it to spread.

4. Bake for 10 minutes or until a pale golden colour. Dust with caster sugar and transfer to a wire cooling rack with a palette knife. Serve piled with fresh strawberries and whipped cream.

Cook's notes

Store the biscuits in an airtight container for up to a week. This recipe is even better if you use vanilla sugar – this can be bought or made by leaving caster sugar in a large jar with a couple of vanilla pods in it. After you have used some sugar top up the jar again with more. You can also use a whole vanilla pod to flavour recipes like custards or compôtes; after use wash and dry the pod and return it to the jar of sugar.

vanilla thins

Makes: 40   Preparation time: 15 minutes   Cooking time: 15 minutes   Freezing: Recommended

The dough for these light and crispy biscuits keeps for a week in the fridge – simply slice off a few at a time for freshly baked biscuits to order! They are delicious served with creamy desserts like the Peach Melba Fool (page 49) or the Cookies and Cream Ice Cream (page 47) or on their own with coffee.

225 g (8 oz) butter

225 g (8 oz) caster sugar

3 teaspoons vanilla essence

1 vanilla pod, halved lengthways

1 large egg

300 g (10½ oz) plain flour

1 teaspoon baking powder

½ teaspoon salt

1. Put the butter, sugar and vanilla essence into the processor bowl fitted with the knife blade, scrape in the seeds from the vanilla pod and cream together for a few minutes until pale and fluffy.

2. Add the egg and mix in well. Add the flour, baking powder and salt and process briefly until evenly combined.

3. Turn out onto a floured work surface and knead together lightly for 1 minute then put on a piece of greaseproof paper and roll into a cylinder shape.

4. Put the dough in the fridge for at least 2 hours, preferably overnight.

5. To bake, preheat the oven to Gas Mark 5/190°C/375°F. Slice off thin rounds from the dough as required and place on baking sheets lined with baking parchment. Bake for 10 minutes or until golden brown and set. Cool slightly on the baking sheet before transferring to a wire cooling rack.

Variations

Try adding 1 tablespoon of ground ginger instead of the vanilla essence and seeds or 1 tablespoon of ground cinnamon.

moist chocolate cake

Ⓥ Serves: 4 Preparation time: 15 minutes Cooking time: 20 minutes Freezing: Recommended

The ultimate in chocolate desserts – this is a cross between a cake and a mousse. It's made with the best-quality dark chocolate and ground almonds and it has a slightly moist squidgy centre.

4 eggs
225 g (8 oz) caster sugar
2 drops of vanilla essence
150 g (5½ oz) dark chocolate (preferably 70% cocoa solids)
125 g (4½ oz) unsalted butter
50 ml (2 fl oz) water
25 g (1 oz) plain flour
50 g (2 oz) ground almonds
icing sugar or cocoa powder, to dust
whipped cream, to serve

1. Preheat the oven to Gas Mark 3/170°C/320°F. Grease and line an 18 cm (7-inch) loose-bottomed cake tin.

2. Using the whisk attachment whisk together the eggs, sugar and vanilla essence for 2 minutes until very light and fluffy.

3. Meanwhile, put the chocolate, butter and water in a large bowl, and heat over a saucepan of simmering water, but do not stir. When they are all melted, stir gently together.

4. Using a metal spoon, gently but thoroughly fold the creamed mixture into the chocolate mixture. Stir in the almonds and the flour. Pour into the tin and bake for 20 minutes. When cooked remove from the tin and place on a cooling rack. Dust with icing sugar or cocoa and serve with whipped cream.

Cook's note
This cake will sink when it comes out of the oven. It is meant to be slightly gooey in the middle with a crunchy crust on the outside, quite like a good chocolate brownie!

chunky chocolate chip cookies

Ⓥ **Makes: 18** **Preparation time: 15 minutes** **Cooking time: 20 minutes** **Freezing: Not Recommended**

Generous chunks of chocolate and oats give these cookies a really chunky bite.

200 g (7 oz) plain chocolate
125 g (4½ oz) unsalted butter
150 g (5½ oz) plain flour
½ teaspoon baking powder
75 g (2¾ oz) porridge oats
1 egg
125 g (4½ oz) light muscovado sugar

1. Preheat the oven to Gas Mark 4/180°C/350°F. Line 2 baking sheets with baking parchment.

2. Put the chocolate in the processor bowl fitted with the knife blade. Pulse until you have quite large chunks. Tip the chocolate onto a plate and reserve. Place the butter, flour, baking powder and porridge oats in the processor bowl. Process for 30 seconds or until the mixture resembles fine breadcrumbs.

3. Add the egg and sugar to the bowl and pulse until well combined. Lastly add the chocolate and pulse again until just combined. Be careful not to overprocess.

4. Using a spoon put piles of the mixture onto the baking sheets, keeping them well apart to allow room for spreading. Flatten each pile slightly with the back of a fork.

5. Bake for 15–20 minutes or until they are pale golden. Leave on the baking sheet for 2 minutes to cool before lifting the cookies onto a wire cooling rack. Serve dusted with icing sugar.

Variations
Try adding 50 g (2 oz) peanuts with the chocolate chunks. The cookies are also delicious made with milk and/or white chocolate.

baklava with rosewater syrup

ⓥ **Makes: about 16 pieces** **Preparation time: 15 minutes** **Cooking time: 20 minutes** **Freezing: Not Recommended**

Using shop-bought filo pastry and your Kenwood processor this fragrant Middle Eastern dessert can be made in minutes. Home-made baklava is very different from most of the too-sweet shop-bought versions.

For the syrup:

450 g (1 lb) granulated sugar

300 ml (½ pint) water

2 tablespoons rosewater syrup

For the baklava:

350 g (12 oz) pistachio nuts

150 g (5½ oz) icing sugar

1 tablespoon ground cardamom

150 g (5½ oz) unsalted butter, melted

18 sheets of filo pastry

icing sugar, to dust

1. Preheat the oven to Gas Mark 3/170°C/320°F. Heat the granulated sugar with the water until boiling. Simmer for 10 minutes and then stir in the rosewater and leave to cool.

2. Fit the knife blade to the bowl and chop the pistachios to the texture of fine breadcrumbs. Add the icing sugar and cardamom and pulse to mix.

3. Brush a baking sheet with a little melted butter. Layer 6 sheets of filo pastry on top, brushing melted butter between each. Spread over half the nut mixture then cover with 6 more sheets of pastry, again brushing each one with melted butter.

4. Top the pastry with the remaining nut mixture, then finish with 6 more buttered filo layers. Cut the layers diagonally into strips and then again the other way to make diamond-shaped pieces. Bake for 20 minutes.

5. When the baklava is cooked leave it to cool slightly in the tray, then remove to a plate with a palette knife. Drizzle over the rosewater syrup and serve dusted with icing sugar.

Cook's note
Baklava will keep for a week in an airtight container.

breads

Whether you've a few minutes or a few hours to spare you can make wonderful home-made bread with the help of your Kenwood food processor. This chapter contains easy recipes for making a range of breads from quick Irish Soda Bread, Spicy Griddled Flatbreads to moist Apple and Cinnamon Scones. And if you have a little more time to allow for rising, why not have a go at making Olive and Sun-dried Tomato Focaccia?

olive and sun-dried tomato focaccia bread

ⓥ Serves: 4–6 Preparation time: 10 minutes plus 30 minutes rising time Cooking time: 10–15 minutes Freezing: Not Recommended

Made the cheat's way with bought pizza base mix in the Kenwood, this light and tasty Italian bread is delicious sliced in half and filled with countless different sandwich combinations.

225 ml (8 fl oz) warm water

2 teaspoons active dried yeast

1 teaspoon sugar

2 × 150 g (5½ oz) packets of pizza base mix

25 g (1 oz) pitted olives, sliced

25 g (1 oz) sundried tomatoes, soaked for 5 minutes in warm water, drained and sliced finely

1 tablespoon olive oil

1. In a small mixing bowl combine the warm water, yeast and sugar and leave for 15 minutes until frothy. Oil a 28 × 18 cm (11 × 7-inch) shallow baking tin.

2. Put the pizza base mix into the processor bowl fitted with the dough attachment. With the machine running, pour the frothed yeast mixture down the feed tube and mix to a soft dough. Knead for 2–3 minutes in the machine until smooth in texture.

3. Press into the prepared baking tin, pushing the dough into the corners. Cover with oiled clingfilm and leave to rise in a warm place for about 30 minutes or until doubled in height.

4. Meanwhile preheat the oven to Gas Mark 7/220°C/425°F. Make dimples all over the surface of the risen dough with your fingers and sprinkle with the olives and sun-dried tomatoes and drizzle with the olive oil.

5. Bake for 10–15 minutes until golden.

Variations
Sprinkle the bread with sea salt and a little fresh chopped rosemary or thyme instead of the olives and tomatoes. To make a sweet focaccia add 1 tablespoon of sugar to the dry pizza base mix before adding the yeast, and also sprinkle a little demerara sugar over the finished dough before cooking.

spicy griddled flatbreads

**Ⓥ Makes: 14 Preparation time: 15 minutes Cooking time: 30 minutes (1 minute on each side)
Freezing: Not Recommended**

These flatbreads are made quickly and easily in the Kenwood and the dough doesn't contain any yeast so there is no rising involved. They are the perfect accompaniment to soups or curries or with cheese and chutneys, like Spicy Tomato Chutney (page 21).

300 g (10½ oz) plain wholemeal flour

100 g (3½ oz) plain flour

2 teaspoons salt

2 teaspoons ground cumin

1 teaspoon ground coriander

½ teaspoon chilli powder

250 ml (9 fl oz) water

1 tablespoon olive oil

1. Put all the dry ingredients in the bowl fitted with the dough tool. With the motor running, gradually add the water until a dough forms.

2. Turn the dough out onto a floured work surface and knead gently together. Divide the dough into 14 equal pieces.

3. Roll each piece into a ball in your hands, then roll out each ball to form a 5 mm (¼-inch) thick round or oval. Brush one side with a little olive oil.

4. Cook oil-side down on a hot griddle pan, barbecue or dry frying pan for 1 minute. Brush the top with oil and turn over for another minute until the bread is puffed and golden.

irish soda bread

Ⅴ **Serves 4:** **Preparation time: 10 minutes** **Cooking time: 40 minutes** **Freezing: Not Recommended**

This recipe is from *Ballymaloe House* in southern Ireland. This bread is quick to make because it doesn't have to be left to rise. It has a very distinctive soda bread taste and texture which requires lashings of butter!

450 g (1 lb) plain flour
1 teaspoon sugar
1 teaspoon salt
1 teaspoon bicarbonate of soda
350–425 ml (12–15 fl oz) buttermilk or 500 g (1 lb 2 oz) plain live yogurt

1. Preheat the oven to Gas Mark 8/230°C/450°F. Lightly grease then flour a baking sheet.

2. Sieve the dry ingredients into the bowl fitted with the dough tool. Mix together. Pour in most of the buttermilk and mix, adding more buttermilk if necessary to make a soft dough.

3. Turn the dough out onto a floured work surface and with floured hands pat it into a circle about 4 cm (1½ inches) deep.

4. Put onto the baking sheet and, using a floured knife, cut a shallow cross right across the dough. Bake for 10 minutes then reduce the oven temperature to Gas Mark 6/200°C/400°F and bake for a further 30 minutes.

Cook's note
To check the bread is cooked tap the bottom and it should sound hollow.

apple and cinnamon scones

ⓥ **Makes: about 20 scones**   **Preparation time: 10 minutes**   **Cooking time: 8–10 minutes**
Freezing: Not Recommended

Use your Kenwood to make these soft and tasty little scones and they can be ready to eat in 20 minutes.

225 g (8 oz) eating apples, peeled, cored and quartered
225 g (8 oz) self-raising flour
1 teaspoon baking powder
2 teaspoons ground cinnamon
50 g (1¾ oz) butter, cut into pieces
50 g (1¾ oz) caster sugar
1 egg, beaten
2 tablespoons golden granulated sugar

1. Preheat the oven to Gas Mark 7/220°C/425°F. Grate the apple with the coarse shredding disc and put into a bowl.

2. Put the flour with the baking powder and cinnamon into the bowl fitted with the knife blade. Add the butter and the grated apple and process until the mixture comes together in a soft dough.

3. Turn the dough out onto a floured work surface and with floury hands press it out until it is 2.5 cm (1 inch) thick. Use a floured 5 cm (2-inch) round cutter and cut out the scones. Place them on a piece of baking parchment on a baking tray, dust with flour and place the scones on the paper.

4. Brush the tops with beaten egg and sprinkle with the sugar.

5. Bake for 8–10 minutes until light golden and well risen. Transfer at once onto a wire cooling rack to cool. Serve with butter and cream or jam.

Cook's note
The secret to soft and airy scones is to handle the dough very lightly and for a minimum of time.

index

apple and cinnamon scones 62
apples 10

baklava 57
banana cake 50
bananas 10
batter 8, 13
bean and rosemary soup 24
biscuits 10
bread 8, 19, 59, 60, 61
breadcrumbs 10

cabbage 10
cakes 8, 16
candied peel 10
carrots 10
celeriac 10
celery 10
cheese 10
chicken satays 35
chillies 10
chocolate cake 54
chocolate chip cookies 56
chutney, spicy tomato 21
cookies and cream ice cream 47
coulis 8
courgette, cheddar and dijon tart 27
courgettes 10
crab and noodle salad 38
cucumbers 11

dips, savoury 9

eggs 11
empanadas, spanish 44
escalopes of pork 31

fennel and parmesan salad 28
fennel bulbs 11
fish cakes, thai 37
fish goujons 39
flatbreads 60
focaccia bread 59

garlic 11
garlic butter 8

herbs 11
hummus 20

ice cream 9, 47
ice lollies 9

jansson's temptation 41

lamb kofta 33
leeks 11
lemon polenta cake 51

mayonnaise 9
meat 11
mexican tortillas 32
milkshakes 9
mushrooms 11

nuts 11

omelettes, stir-fry vegetable 42
onion bhajis 29
onions 11

parsnips 11
pastry, choux 15
pastry, shortcrust 9, 14
pea and mint soup 23
peach melba fool 49
pear and almond tarts 48
pears 11
pesto 9
pizza dough 17
polenta cake, lemon 51
potato rösti florentine 43
potatoes 11
purées 8, 9

radishes 11
roasted tomato soup 25

satays, chicken 35
sauces 8
scones 9, 62
smoothies 9
soda bread 61
sorbets 9
soups 9, 25
sponge, victoria 16
stir-fry vegetable omelettes 42
strawberry shortcakes 52
swedes 11

tomato soup, roasted 25
tomatoes 11
turnips 11

vanilla thins 53
victoria sponge cake 16
vinaigrette dressings 9